THIS BOOK BELONGS TO

GEOFF LYNN May 81

THE JOY OF FOOTBALL

MADE IN JAPAN

THE JOY OF FOOTBALL

MADE IN JAPAN

Eric Nicol & Dave More

Hurtig Publishers

Hurtig Publishers Ltd.
10560 105 Street
Edmonton, Alberta

Canadian Cataloguing in Publication Data

Nicol, Eric, 1919-
    The joy of football

    ISBN 0-88830-183-9

    1. Football, Canadian* — Anecdotes, facetiae,
satire, etc.   2. Canadian wit and humor (English).*
I. More, Dave. II. Title.

GV948.N52   796.33'5'0207   C80-091007-9

Printed and bound in Canada
by John Deyell Company

CONTENTS

THE EVOLUTION
OF FOOTBALL
(A Half-hour Later
in Newfoundland)

Origin of the three-point stance

Piltdown man

Touchdown man

In November 1979 a group of anthropologists digging in Africa's famed Olduvai Gorge unearthed the perfectly preserved skeleton of an ape in whose arm was cradled a coconut. The creature had been killed in mid-stride by a crushing blow to the side of the skull. The find was immediately hailed not only as the missing link between man and the great apes but also as proof that football is at least three million years old. This claim was later challenged when it was found that the ape had lost none of his front teeth and he was wearing an athletic support labelled Tumble Dry.

Nevertheless, we have evidence that football goes back a long way, especially when played against the wind. Cavemen enjoyed this participation sport even after they discovered the club and its healthful effect on cavewomen. All that was needed to play football was a field and a reasonably round object whose hair had been shaved off. Football put the fun back into decapitation.

Most authorities agree that modern football evolved from earlier forms of contact sport, such as being trampled by a herd of elephants. However, in some regions, notably the Deep South of the United States where football is an orthodox religion, it is still unlawful to teach in school the evolutionary theory of football. Belief there remains firm that football was one of the innocent pastimes of the Garden of Eden, the game being lost because of a bad hand-off of the apple, Eve to Adam. It is to defend against this satanic game plan that most American football teams kneel for the pre-game prayer. The Sabbath devotions are less intense among Canadian football teams, probably because the players know that God is watching a game in the States.

Attic Football

Did the Ancient Greeks play football? Some historians, pointing to the Argonauts, say "Yes." (Not the Toronto Argonauts, who are not 2500 years old; they only play that way.) The Argonauts of Greece were the first team to blame a tough travel schedule for failing to bring home the Golden Fleece, an early form of season's ticket.

Other scholars cite the sacking of Troy, Troy being a quarterback for the Trojans of Ilium. The Greeks won that hotly-contested game by hiding their team inside a wooden horse, which the Trojans drew offside, resulting in a penalty: the city was burned and the ground ploughed and salted — the forerunner of today's Grey Cup.

Although the Achilles' heel is still a vulnerable part of the football player's anatomy, the major influence of Greek mythology on the game undoubtedly was Bacchus or Dionysus, god of wine and back-to-back orgies. The full Bacchus, and the demigod half-Bacchus, created the running game. The bacchanalian frenzy of tearing the victim to pieces in the open field introduced the special team. The vital role of the grape in football has changed only in that Bacchus is now called Schenley, Carling, or Molson. The beer can is held sacred among devotees, and the brandishing of the thyrsus by wild, wild women survives with the pom-pom girls.

So much for legend. On the more factual side we know that the Romans adopted football from Greece because they needed something to put into the Colosseum that offered better betting odds than the Lions *vs.* the Christians. The Romans introduced the element of kicking, but it was several hundred years before they thought of the football. By then it was too late, the Roman Empire having been taken over by primitive Goths who couldn't figure out a way of pulling the football jersey over the horns on their helmets.

The northerners did however contribute the words from which *football* derives, namely *foot* and, to put it plainly, *ball*. *Foot* comes from the Old English *fot*, the name given to the part of the leg turned up at the ankle, and *ball* comes from the even Older English *bealluc*, or testes, located at the opposite end of the leg. Etymologically, therefore, *football* means using one appendage to boot another, resulting in the Middle Ages.

Middle-Aged Football

Not surprisingly, Old English football was banned several times during the Middle Ages because it was too brutal, had no rules, and was wiping out more Britons than were the Crusades. British football almost originated in Scotland when the Scots invented the haggis and were undecided whether to kick it or eat it. They eventually ate it, setting back football several hundred years, during which Scots became emotionally involved with a smaller, harder ball that had proved indigestible, thus inventing golf.

In England, where food was more plentiful, the masses played football with undiminished fury as a means of building up their resistance to civilization. At this time civilization was being imported by the Norman French, who played football wearing much shorter shorts and were therefore viewed as perverts.

Britons also wanted nothing to do with Renaissance football, which in Florence took the form of a revival of interest in the human body with both arms missing. The savage Britons were content to continue chasing one another up and down a field in the blood sport for people who couldn't afford a horse.

Victorian Elegance

In the nineteenth century football was adopted by several English public schools that were looking for a forcible way to convince people that they were actually private schools. "Waterloo was won on the playing fields of Eton," said the Duke of Wellington, which was a nice

Vulgarization of rugby

way of saying that Napoleon was too short to play quarterback. (Today Canada has its own Waterloo, a university that fields a football team with brave disregard for the fact that God is on the side with the heaviest linemen.)

At one of these schools, Rugby, a variation on football came into being when a fat boy fell on the ball and squashed it into an oblong shape. To avoid taking the blame, the fat boy picked up the ball and tossed it to another player, who in turn quickly got rid of it to a third player, the process being repeated until the entire team fell on the ball to hide it. Thus was born rugby. Rugby (or rugger) was an upper-class football in which the player was permitted to handle the ball and run with it because his father had money.

Other English exclusive schools quickly welcomed

rugby, the team colours providing a basis for the Old School Tie, a much-needed means by which an English gentleman recognizes another English gentleman without having to speak to him. To this day, in vestigial parts of the Empire such as New Zealand, Fiji, and Vancouver Island, rugby is the best preparation for leadership next to owning a whale's tooth.

The old form of football, played with the feet and therefore beneath contempt, became known as "soccer", from Association Football, so called because only persons with no breeding would associate with it. Soccer became the working man's game, spreading to eastern Europe, becoming both communist and catholic, and failing to be regarded as a reliable source of officer material.

Anxious to have their students mistaken for gentry, the first universities and private schools of Canada fielded rugger teams. Boys who wanted to play soccer were given to understand that soccer was a type of self-abuse, leading possibly to blindness.

In contrast, the Americans of New England played Association Football from colonial times because all the gentlemen were in the Deep South. Development of football in the United States was also delayed by the Civil War, in which both sides managed to get much the same effect by scrimmaging over a cannonball.

Formation of the Rugby Football Union brought a new element into the game: rules. Previously the only rule had been to start the game with fifteen men a side and play till there were only eleven, owing to fatalities. Most of the new rules were designed to make football

*Introduction of
broken-field running*

safer. The substitution rule, for example, made it possible to remove the body of a player from the field before another player tripped over it and hurt himself.

In addition to adopting Rugby Union rules, Montreal's McGill University was able to take advantage of the abundance of timber in Canada to develop football goal posts that extended above the crossbar — a clean break with grass hockey. A celebrated game of football between McGill and Harvard gave the Americans their first experience with the broader education provided by tackling with the arms instead of the legs, as well as with a system of scoring that showed the advantage of learning to count above ten. Football never looked back.

WHAT YOU NEED
TO PLAY FOOTBALL
(Besides Faith
in an Afterlife)

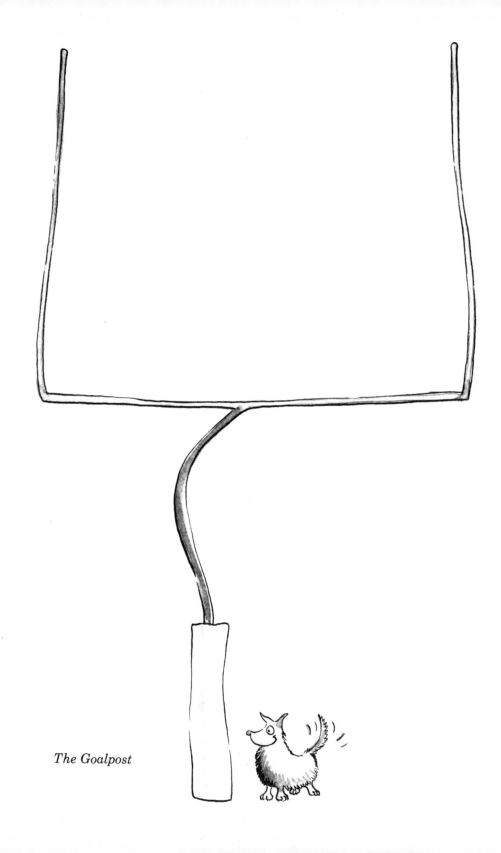

The Goalpost

 *Field*

The field is almost essential to the game of football. Some players contend that they can have a pretty good game in a smaller space, such as a hot tub. But is it football? More likely it is "touch" football, an effeminate version of the game in which there is no incentive to fall down unless you step on the soap. In normal football nearly all the players fall down on every play, and experience has shown that the best thing to fall down on is a field (unless the game is co-ed).

Originally the field was a pasture shared with cows and sheep. This helped to develop broken-field running, or the ability to swerve around objects that do not enhance one's charm. Today, many football fields are still natural sod, particularly those of colleges and universities that value mud as an immersion program. The grass field helps to sustain the mystic relationship between man and the soil, and is also important to television commercials for detergents that get out ground-in dirt.

The professional football field however is more likely to be a synthetic — machine-washable, no ironing, hold the bleach. The advantage of the field of man-made rug is that it eliminates the need to replace the divot. Stopping in the middle of a run to replace the divot can slow down the game. Also, as the player is being carried off the field, it is nice if his jersey is clean enough for the spectators to be able to tell which team he belonged to. Aside from causing more injuries that leave the player crippled for life, artificial turf is wonderfully trouble-free.

Whether it is is mowed or sewed, the regulation field is 110 yards long (100 yards in the United States because of higher property values). How long will the Canadian football field be when it goes metric? No one knows. With the field marked off by lines ten metres apart, instead of ten yards, it becomes about ten yards longer and pushes the goal posts up into the cheap seats. Many end zones are too small already. The loss of another five yards at each end will afford the player scoring a touchdown an even briefer period of euphoria before he crashes into the brick wall. The metric field will however make the game more readily understood by Frenchmen, should football ever replace sex.

The entire playing area of the field is bounded by sidelines painted far enough apart to prevent the rival coaches from being able to clutch one another by the throats. Anything that happens outside these lines is "out of bounds", if not actually depraved. Here the

Sideline play

players are provided with benches to bleed on. Players are discouraged from bringing their own deck chairs. The atmosphere along the sidelines is supposed to be that created by wounded infantrymen in the Crimean War before Florence Nightingale found the lamp and invented night games.

The Goal Posts (One Pair)

These structures serve two main purposes: A. they give the football player something to aim for in life; and B. they show that one end of the field is much the same as the other end. A minor function is to cause acute anxiety in the field goal kicker. (Football is the opposite of the medical profession in that it provides an ailment for every specialist.) Finally, the goal posts are needed in a kicking try for the point after touchdown. When success-

21

ful, this is called "a conversion", and is as close to a religious experience as the kicker is apt to get. For this reason the goal posts may be thought of as the visible expression of football's power to convert the heathen: two slender arms thrust towards Heaven, beseeching the Almighty to block that kick.

The Uniform

In no other game is the uniform so important as in football. The uniform makes the player look much bigger than he actually is. This gives him the sense of being invincible that is essential to his being dumb enough to go out on the field.

The completely-accoutred football player is a magnificent inverted pyramid with a dome on the blunt end. He is a heroic sight as he trots off the field with his helmet under his arm, especially if his head is still in it. He is a modern knight in armour. The same athlete who looks quite ordinary in street clothes becomes, in the metamorphosis in the dressing room, a gladiator of fearsome aspect, his mere glance turning a woman to warm tapioca and making other men consider a career change to full-time eunuch.

What are the components of the football uniform? Starting at the more vulnerable end, the feet, we have *the shoes*. The beginner often neglects his football shoes, believing that because they are at ground level no one will notice them. This is a mistake. The football player spends much of his time cartwheeling through the air, so that spectators cannot but observe that his footwear is of inferior quality.

Many professional players favour low-cut shoes because they are sexier than boots. The football boots worn by all players during the early years of the game do provide extra support for the ankle but can heighten resemblance to a lady wrestler. High heels are definitely not recommended. Regardless of how runtish the player is, and how much he resents being called "Lofty", his wearing elevator shoes — except possibly for evening games — will shorten the life of his body.

Next, *socks*. Does it matter that a player's socks fall down during a game? Indeed it does. Professional football players are severely disciplined for playing with their socks at half-mast unless a member of the team

has died. Most coaches become enraged if they are taken literally when they yell "Pull up your socks!" They insist on pantyhose, garter belts, or over-developed calves to prevent socks from losing their poise. Younger players should however avoid wearing garters that cut off the circulation, as they will develop varicose veins and have to wear support hose.

Tightness can be an even more serious problem with the football player's *pants*. Several theories are offered as to why football pants are so snug. One is that it cuts down wind resistance. However, players wear tight pants even when there is no wind, or when the wind is behind them and loose bloomers would actually boost their speed. Another belief is that the tight pants leave

The shoes

the tackler nothing to hold on to but the church of his choice.

According to game historians, the tight britches stem from the style of the Elizabethan dandy who "made a leg" in order to impress the opposite sex (women, unless otherwise posted — see the deleted chapter "Football as Foreplay"). Form-fitting knickers have traditionally clad the cock of the walk, for example the Spanish toreador, there apparently being a connection between walking tall and pants too tight in the crotch.

Thanks to new stretch materials, it is possible for the football player to combine very tight pants and bending over in the huddle without having an accident that gets him arrested. The pants also accommodate

The socks

knee pads, thigh pads, kidney pads, and a gold waistlet for the player who wants his good-luck charms down where they will do the most good.

What about *the double cup*? First, this is not a bra. (The male football player who is worried about his cleavage should seek professional advice.) The double cup, and its optimistic alternative the single cup, help to prevent the kind of mishap which otherwise necessitates the rest of the team forming a cordon around the stricken player to screen him from the view of 50,000 people until he has stopped rolling around clutching himself. To suffer on the field, delaying the game and wasting a time-out, is a form of self-indulgence. Unless the player has a very high threshold of pain and is able to writhe quickly to the sideline, though suddenly dis-

The pants

qualified from ever having children, he has an obligation to the team to protect sensitive parts of his anatomy. Or, for that matter, his head.

The helmet is by far the most essential part of the football player's gear. Like Don Quixote, he needs his helmet in order to convince himself that what he is doing is meaningful. If he forgets to put his pants on, it is an oversight, but without his helmet *the football player is naked*.

Originally the function of the football helmet was to mitigate the physical effects of being kicked in the head, or of having one's face stepped on by a 250-pound lineman. For this reason the helmet was made up of a solid part and a face mask, the face mask hampering vision somewhat and encouraging players to put the helmet on

The double cup

backwards. Construction of the football helmet has been much improved since the days when it was a leather commode. Light yet strong materials used today make it possible for the helmet to take an impact equivalent to that of a runaway cement truck without damage to the skull, though all the player's toenails fall off.

The player should always raise the face mask before spitting. This is one of several uses of the helmet as an extension of the player's personality. Others are:

- flinging open the chin strap to prevent the mouth from being trapped in the cage with a raging expletive;
- sitting on the helmet, on the sideline, to amplify seismic vibrations;

The helmet,
et al.

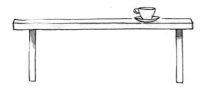

al.

Getting involved

- slamming the helmet to the ground to indicate disagreement with an official's call.

The helmet also bears the insignia of the team. This helps the player to know which side he is playing for, without having to ask a policeman.

From this it is clear that for the football player his helmet holds the same mystic symbolism as the plumed hat held for Cyrano de Bergerac, who in Rostand's play cries *"Mon panache!"* after being fatally crowned by a falling flower pot. Indeed some football linemen have stuck a feather in their helmets, until asked to remove it because it was making the opposing lineman sneeze.

The Coach

Every football team worthy of the name has a coach. In fact most teams go through more coaches than a CPR trainman. Even a team of small boys playing in a vacant lot has a coach, whether it wants one or not. Thousands of fathers and other fat men find an outlet for community service in bullying little kids. Coaching a football team allows them to do this without being arrested for child abuse. The football coach therefore fills a need in a society that has done away with feeding children to a stone idol.

I

The professional team has a variety of coaches, as a matter of pride if nothing else. The most conspicuous of these coaches is the head coach. This is the coach who coaches the head. Working under the head coach are the back coach, the front coach, the belly coach, the unmentionable coach, the legs coach, and — lowly but with dignity — the feet coach.

Ideally there should be a coach for every position on the team, including a coach coach. The coach coach

II

helps the head coach prepare statements for the media, before, after, and between games. Since much of the head coach's time is spent in press interviews, explaining why his team is taking its opponents seriously, the coach coach studies the films of the interviews, and shows the head coach where his humility broke down, points out unsuccessful attempts to tackle a polysyllable, and diagrams moves to block the hypothetical question without slapping the hand over the mouth.

III

No amount of coaching can teach the head coach the most important part of his position, which is to show no emotion during the game. It is something a coach is born with: the ability to stand quite still, without being rigid, on the sideline and to keep the same expression regardless of whether his team is thirty points ahead or behind. The coach who shows that he is only human obviously belongs in a minor league. Unless the coach has mastered body language, his players may notice little things like his tearing his hair out, his lying on the ground beating his fists on the turf, or his committing hara-kiri. And this can make his players feel insecure.

Some head coaches who are unable to hide their emotions have tried having their faces frozen by their dentists before the game. The anaesthetic usually begins to wear off, however, by half-time, so that for the last

IV

two quarters half the face is stony while the other half is contorted by hysteria. If anything, this mien is more disconcerting to the team and the fans than is the coach's weeping during the coin toss.

The players look to the head coach not only for emotional stability during the game but also for plays sent in from the sideline with a player whose attention span can be trusted. The head coach receives messages from

above, some on his head-set, others as a direct transmission from the Almighty. He also consults charts provided by his assistants, estimating the percentile chances of success of a given play against a given team on a given day with a given degree of humidity. For this reason we may conclude that the head football coach of tomorrow will be a computer-robot. Indeed IBM has already made such a drone (called "Rocky") which formulates the perfect game plan. The robot coach is ready for the market but for one bug: when he chews gum, his knees light up.

The robot will simplify one of the problems of the head coach, namely being fired when his team loses. Coaching in the CFL or NFL is a Cinderella story: when the clock runs out, the coach turns into a pumpkin. The robot coach will reduce the distress of his having to be fired. When the team loses two games in a row, the head coach simply self-destructs.

The Football

Last (and probably least) item of equipment needed to play the game is the football. Some football players play out their entire careers without having fired a ball in anger. Most rarely touch the ball. A few have died doubting its existence. Nevertheless the player should become familiar with what the ball looks like lest he pick it up on the field and try to turn it in to the Lost and Found.

The football gives the player something to do with his hands when he is not busy with his normal occupa-

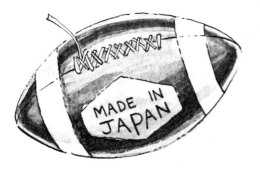

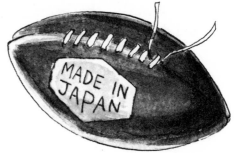

A Canadian football   *An American football*

tion of dismembering an opponent. And of course the kick-off and the punt are more meaningful when the kicker's foot is able to make contact with the ball.

Originally the football was made of pigskin. This helped Jewish mothers to talk their sons into playing the violin instead. Today's football however is kosher. A quarterback such as Joe Namath can "eat the ball" without compromising his religious faith.

The ball used in American football is smaller than in Canadian football. It is the lesser of two ovals. The Canadian ball is larger so that it is easier to find in the mud. It is also harder to throw and to kick, in keeping with the Canadian character, which distrusts anything that is easily moved when sober.

Anti-inflation boards to the contrary, when in play the football should be pumped up. (Not to be confused with the Howard Cosell-ism, "The entire team is pumped up for this game." Other means are used to pump up a team, and the pressure is tested by squeezing the referee.)

37

Finally, the beginning football player should understand that there will come a time in his career when he will no longer automatically make the team just because it is his football. Professional football teams such as the Dallas Cowboys often own two or more balls.

PREPARING
THE BODY

The Wishbone

Football is the most dangerous game you can play without getting into bed. Ask yourself:

Am I Physical?

The wonderful thing about football is that anyone can play the game, provided he is over six feet tall and weighs more than two hundred pounds.

But size is not important in football unless the player is excessively dominated by the will to live. There are quite a number of pro football players who are under five foot six. True, when they started playing they were *six* foot six. Repeatedly colliding head first with a goal post can modify the height of even the tallest person.

Is it a handicap in football to have a neck? Frankly, yes. A neck is just one more part of the body for an opposing player to tackle — "clothes line", to use the technical term. If you can see your Adam's apple without removing your undershirt you may be in trouble.

Ideally, the football player's head is joined directly to his torso. When he wears a bow tie, it slips up under his nose. If he does have a neck, it must be a massive column of the same diameter as his head. Projecting ears are taboo. For the same reason the player should have no hips. A generous pelvic basin is fine for gestation, but as a rule the football player does not have nine months in which to produce. If your pants stay up without a belt, therefore, you may be better off playing another game, one in which hips are not hazardous to health.

In contrast, the football player cannot have too much shoulder. Shoulder pads can make up for a certain amount of deficiency in this part of the body, but eventually the player will have to take a shower, and his lack of shoulders may be noticed.

Shoulders are needed for blocking and tackling, and they give the player something to fall on besides his head. Generally speaking, a separated shoulder is preferable to a separated face.

Should a football player wear glasses? Only if he has an eyesight problem. Otherwise spectacles are an affectation. Professional players usually wear contact lenses because looking for one in the grass provides a pleasant respite from the hurly-burly of the game.

Now, what about legs? It is impossible to discuss legs without touching upon the subject of physical specialization in football. If you have listened to football commentators you know that they refer to the running back as having enormous thighs — "as big around as an ordinary man's waist". If your thigh is as big around as an ordinary man's wrist — reconsider. You may be more effective in another position: chartered accountant, for instance.

Just as a running back needs legs sturdy enough to keep churning ahead long after the rest of his body has been brought to a halt ("second effort"), so does the pass receiver benefit from great height and unusually long arms. You can easily test yourself as a potential tight end. Wrap your arms around your chest. If your fingertips touch at the back, you have the required reach. Unfortunately the embrace may start a love affair from which it is difficult to extract yourself. There is no easy road to physical fitness.

Finally, the hands. The advantage of long and muscular arms is largely offset if they come to a bad end. The beginning football player should therefore study his hands objectively. Is the thumb opposable? That is, does your thumb get lonesome when lined up on the opposite side of the ball from the rest of the fingers? Do you find it easier to grip things with your tail?

If you are to play pass receiver it is vital to have "good hands", regardless of how clever you are at leaping up and catching the ball with your mouth, and romping back to the thrower to drop the ball at his feet. Watching too many Lassie films can distort your view of hands. You must be able to hang on to the ball while being hit. One way to assess your ability in this respect is to stand in the middle of a railway track, the hands holding the ball firmly above the head as you are struck

Illegal use of hands

by a freight train. If you are still clutching the ball when you are carried into the intensive care unit, you may have a future as a punt return man.

The player should not be discouraged because he has only one pair of hands. He should not emulate the backfield coach who worships Siva, the Hindu god of destruction, whose four arms make him ideal for flanker. It would be nice to be able simultaneously to catch the ball and tackle an opponent and still have enough fingers free to count the house, but developing multiple limbs is not worth the risk of being limited to scuttling sideways.

Those players on the team who do not handle the ball can, of course, do without hands altogether. Linemen tape their hands along with the rest of their forearms in order to resist the temptation to hold something, an act for which his team may be penalized. (It may be difficult to imagine why anybody would want to hold an opposing lineman, except his mother, but as you get older you will find that the passionate impulse is unpredictable.)

These, then, are the parts of the body involved in football. Ideally, they should all be connected together, at least to begin with. It makes it easier to count how many players are on the field.

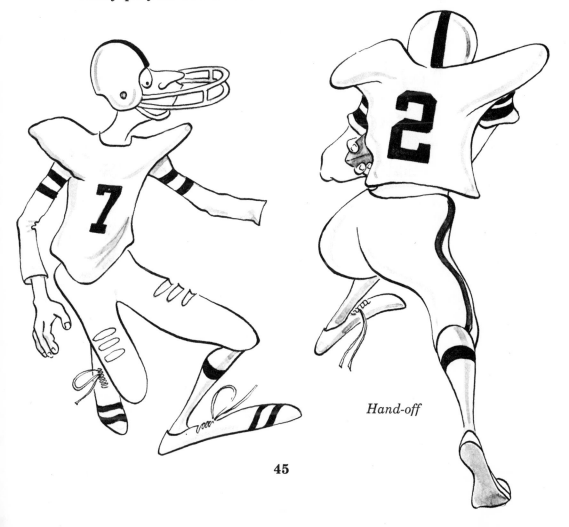

Hand-off

45

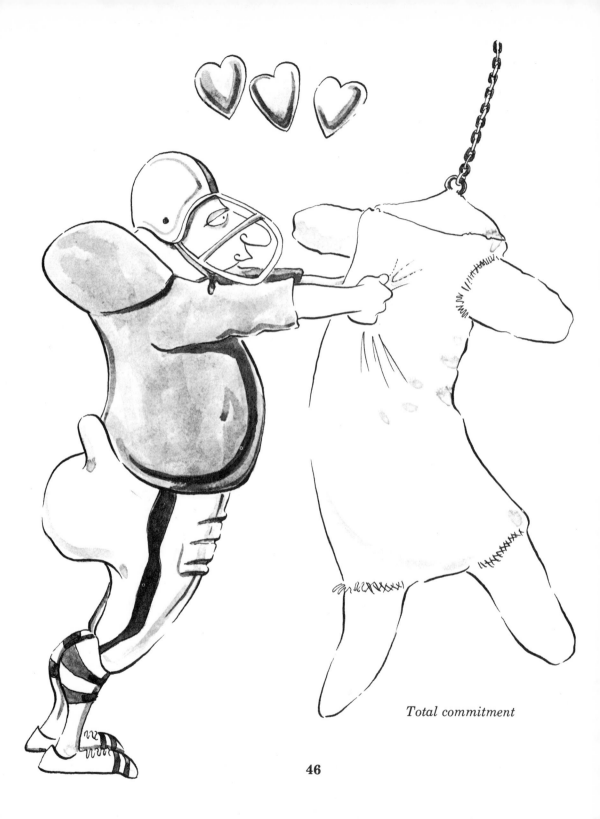

Total commitment

Am I Mental?

Is it an advantage for the football player to have a brain? This question is argued pro and con, as well as pro and amateur.

On the negative side, a player is handicapped when his cranium is occupied by a rather delicate organ that cannot sustain a simple skull fracture without his losing consciousness. We are all familiar with the tedious delays caused when a player has "had his bell rung". The trainer must trot onto the field to ask the blank-eyed victim his name, and where he is. In some respects it is better if the player does not know his name or where he is, even when fully conscious. The game is speeded up, and the team's medical staff is relieved of the responsibility of distinguishing between a slight concussion, permanent brain damage, and Goodnight, Irene.

Another drawback to having a brain is that the football player may be tempted to think for himself. In football more than in any other game, success depends upon the coach doing the player's thinking for him. In baseball, for example, the player can enjoy periods of rumination, paced by chewing his cud. But in football the action is so sudden that, like Pavlov's dogs, the player must react automatically to a signal. The message goes directly from the ear to the legs, bypassing both the cerebellum and the Montreal post office.

The player who catches himself thinking for himself, during drills, should make a clean breast of the matter to his coach. It is possible that something can be done to correct the condition — a lobotomy, or removal of that part of the brain that controls movements more complex than waving bye-bye.

Against these arguments favouring the player whose cranial cavity is filled with Silly Putty must be measured the plus factors for the player who has a brain, but who thinks in moderation. The player who limits himself to one thought before dinner — no problem. When playing quarterback, he may even be admired for his cunning. The quarterback must be able to "read" the defence or offence, without moving his lips. Any additional signs of intellect — sucking a pipe, say, or perusing a book while sitting on the bench — are not recommended. They infringe on the right of the head coach to be recognized as the higher nervous centre, until such time as he is proven to be located at the opposite end of the spinal column.

Am I American?

Most of the thinking quarterbacks in the Canadian Football League are Americans. In addition, they are Americans who were rejected by the National Football League because they couldn't "cut the mustard". This has led to speculation that American mustard is harder to cut than Canadian mustard. The charge is unfounded. Independent tests of American mustard (Mother Lucifer's) have proved beyond doubt that cutting it requires no more skill or intelligence than does cutting Canadian mustard (Mother Lucifer's of Canada Ltd.).

If the football player can arrange to be from the

The hungry competitor

A compleated pass

United States, well and good. It is certainly something he should talk over with his parents before he is born. For one thing, the average American city is naturally endowed to give the youngster better training for football, especially if he can arrange to be brought up in a poor, black neighborhood. Any kid can learn to run with a ball across an open field, but playing on a busy slum street, dodging taxis, drunks, and muggers, trains the American lad in basic skills in a way that the Canadian cannot duplicate without growing up in a revolving door.

For this reason, the running backs in the CFL are usually American blacks who would be in the starting line-up of an American team if they were bigger, faster, and whiter. Similarly the best defensive backs are imports. Thanks to athletic scholarships awarded by U.S. colleges, they have learned to run backwards as well as forwards. Because few Canadian universities offer athletic scholarships, our players are limited to running in only one direction at a time.

In the lineman positions however the Canadian is every bit the equal of the American, unless the American has recovered sufficiently to be able to play without his crutches. Because the CFL team is required to include a number of Canadians on its roster, the coach, who is planning to become a Canadian unless his team wins enough games for him to jump to coaching in the NFL, must be able to "juggle his linemen". A typical American lineman weighs in excess of two hundred and fifty pounds and turns mean when tossed into the air. The coach is therefore glad to juggle the much lighter

Canadian linemen. What he lacks in impact the Canadian player makes up for by being easier to carry off the field.

Finally — and a feather in our helmet it is — the punter and/or place kicker on a Canadian professional football team is almost always a Canadian. Ounce for ounce, the Canadian can kick the ball farther than can the American, and it speaks well for the extra time he puts in, learning to tie his bootlaces.

STRUCTURED
PLAYTIME

Judgement call

The first rule of football is not to get caught breaking any of the others.

Space does not permit inclusion here of all the rules of football, because the official rule book is bigger than this book and twice as mean. But it is not necessary to know all the rules in order to enjoy the game. Many pro football players enjoy a long and successful career though they know only a couple of basic rules ("Do not put your elbows on the table when eating the ball," and "Never turn your back on anyone, including your grandmother").

The Golden Rule, "Do unto others as you would have them do unto you," does not apply in football, unless you believe that you have a great deal to give to orthopedic surgery. The reason: football is a game of struggle for territory. All beasts fight their own kind for one of two purposes, A. to win a mate, or B. to secure enough territory to keep themselves in food and

Gatorade. Two linemen butting helmets are not unlike a pair of moose battling for the same patch of swamp, except that the moose does not aspire to own his own restaurant.

Thus in football success is measured in yards (metres). It is also "a game of inches" (centimetres). Two of the officials have no other job than to trot back and forth with a chain exactly ten yards long, measuring things. Penalties are assessed in yards. It therefore follows that in order to understand the rules of football the player should have a reasonably clear idea in his mind of how long a yard is. Some novice players think that a yard is a hyper-extended foot. This is wishful thinking. Before he becomes too committed to the impossible dream, every player should borrow his mother's tape measure, mark off three feet, then sit down on a bench and study the distance carefully. He should not get up until he is certain that he will never get the yard confused with the cubit, the furlong, or any other unit of length.

The primary object of the offensive team is to gain ten yards. It does not need to be exactly ten yards. The coach will be just as pleased if the gain is eleven yards, or fifty yards, or indeed any larger distance so long as the team does not leave the country. But the yardage must be obtained in three downs (four downs in American football, which is more possessive than Canadian football and often insanely jealous).

What is a down? If your father tells you that it is a soft material obtained from a duck, he is being less than candid with you in his effort to get you into a manly

Kicker having
intercourse with ball
(averse position)

game. In football the down is almost invariably hard. Some veterans believe that it is the hardest thing a person can run into, unless he attempts intercourse with a brick wall. The dictionary defines a down as an attempt to advance the ball, but this is only a partial description, toned down to avoid alarming women and children. In actual fact, *down,* in football, means the direction in which the body falls, regardless of what other plans it may have had. Football is a game of falling down. To remain upright, after a down, indicates a reluctance to participate. To be buried under a pile of players, on the other hand, is a very sincere form of attention. The person who enjoys company without having to be well liked will find the down amply rewarding.

What happens if the team fails to advance the ball ten yards in three downs? Great disappointment, of course. But the contest is allowed to proceed by the expedient called "turning the ball over". Normally when one turns the ball over, all one finds is the lacing. But when the ball is turned over to the opposing team, the offensive team leaves the field in disgrace, to be replaced by the defensive team, which is larger, fiercer, and totally dedicated to the state of inertia.

When an irresistible force meets an immovable object, it must be Sunday afternoon.

Football is the only game in which the home crowd cheers wildly when there is no discernible movement of the ball. The defensive team may even be given a standing ovation, led by fans whose vision has been blurred by age or choice of beverage and who find it easier to follow the ball when it doesn't go anywhere.

To avoid the humiliation of turning the ball over on downs, the offensive team will often attempt a manoeuvre call *the punt*. The punt is a kick aimed — refreshingly enough — at the ball. It is one of the few times in football when the ball comes into contact with the foot. The other times are the kick-off, the place kick, and the baroque fumble (rare) in which a player accidentally boots the ball instead of the player who is falling on it.

What distinguishes the punt from other kicks at the ball is that the punter (*i.e.,* the player condemned to the punt) does not tee up the ball. This includes winter

Rudimentary punt — Swinemouth-on-Tyne, 1842

Prone or ventral attitude

rules. The reason why he does not tee up the ball to punt is that the opposing team is permitted on the snap of the ball from the centre, to hurl itself forward for the purpose of blocking the punt. The punter therefore has at most four seconds in which to get rid of the ball by whatever means he deems prudent. Should he pause to place the ball on the tee, he will almost certainly discover the fallacy of the expression "better late than never".

On special occasions the punter has the ball held for him by someone whose fingers are expendable. One of these occasions is after his team has scored *a touchdown*. What is a touchdown? The touchdown (or TD) is the most exciting thing that can happen in a football game unless a cheerleader's blouse pops a button. It is scored by taking the ball across the opponent's goal line. Like carrying the bride over the threshold, the touchdown is an emotional experience accompanied by considerable physical activity. The resistance is usually more protracted, but the reward (six points on the scoreboard) has a better chance of being recorded statistically, assuming that the groom does not handle the bride on every carry.

When may a player carry the ball? Any time. So long as the player has given the referee his name and

The Option

A Canadian receiver must keep one *foot in bounds . . .*

the names of his next of kin, and has put his personal affairs in order, he may, as a member of either the offensive or the defensive team, take the ball and run with it until he finds out why his club carries so many extra players.

What possesses a player to take the ball, when all the evidence points to his being better off to take the first plane out of town? The answer: he believes in his

An American receiver must keep both *feet in bounds.*

blocking. The function of the blockers is to thwart the opposing players who have designs on the ball carrier's fair and unpolluted flesh. As diagrammed on the blackboard, the blockers open a path for the ball carrier as wondrous as the Lord's parting the Red Sea for the escape of the Chosen People. Unfortunately, some people are more chosen than others. When a blocker misses his assignment, the ball carrier soon finds himself up to his hips in Red Sea, which would be less serious were he not upside down. It takes a very special kind of player to retain faith in the block, after his own has been knocked off.

Blocking is done against the opposing player who is not carrying the ball. Blocking is sometimes allowed below the waist, or above the waist, but never from the rear. For this reason the player must have some knowledge of anatomy. The waist is not always easy to find on a football player, particularly a lineman. But a player can normally determine his own waist by locating his navel and describing an imaginary line that is too low if it tickles.

Establishing the rear of an opponent is more difficult, especially on the field where decisions must be made quickly. Because most football players can run backwards, their direction of movement is not a positive test of the front end. A more reliable means of recognizing the rear is the *gluteus maximus,* or bum. The physical feature is quite unmistakable on most football players, so that the blocker who sees one looming in his sights should do his best to avoid the penalty for "clipping" by seeking an alternate target, such as the south end of Osoyoos.

Unlike blocking, tackling may be done from front or rear, the player using any part of his body that he considers to be redundant. Being tackled is the price one pays for being found with the football in one's possession. A player should therefore weigh carefully the consequences before he takes the ball, regardless of how politely it is offered. The player accepting the ball should think of it as a hand grenade whose pin was pulled some time ago. That is, he has a very brief interval in which to satisfy the acquisitive instinct. His future health and welfare depend on his A. getting rid of the ball without a formal address of farewell, or B. getting rid of himself, by (i) running out of bounds, or (ii) ringing a small bell while chanting "Unclean! Unclean!" or (iii) direct assumption of the body to Heaven, letting the soul catch up later.

The long bomb

Shoestring tackle

However, if the player is tackled before he can dispose of the ball, the ball is "spotted". The referee spots the ball by saying "Ah-ha, *there* you are, you little rascal!" He then pries the ball out of the lifeless grasp of the ball carrier before rigor mortis makes retrieval difficult, and he places the ball to mark where the body was found. The rival offensive and defensive teams next line up opposite one another, noses pressed against an invisible barrier called the restraining line. This is the no-man's-land for what is often called "the war in the trenches", in which the linemen do their best to recreate the fun and entertainment values of the Battle of Stalingrad.

Once a lineman has dropped into his three-point stance — which may be two hands and a knee, two knees and a hand, an ear and two elbows, or whatever his accident insurance covers — he is not permitted to move until the ball is snapped. Even if a wasp settles on his nose he must remain absolutely motionless. This requires immense self-control. It explains why people who suffer from St. Vitus Dance rarely make the first team. On the other hand you do have a definite advantage if your arms are so long that your knuckles brush the turf even when you are standing upright. All you need to do is remember not to scratch until you are in the huddle.

The Fumble

1. Foreplay

3. Involuntary communion

4. Climax

5. Afterglow

The compleat lineman

THE HUDDLE
AS GROUP THERAPY

The trap play

Football is the only game in which a team holds a formal meeting before every play. This assembly is called *the huddle*. It is hard to overstate the importance of the huddle in football. Despite its superficial resemblance to the rugby scrum or a floating crap game, the football huddle is a much more complex ritual, recalling the Knights of the Round Table in that mystic time before they found a table.

For years the secret rites of the huddle were shrouded in mystery. Players who had taken part in one were reluctant to reveal what went on in the huddle, for fear that the ghost of Knute Rockne would rise up and tie their shoelaces together. In the past decade however a few facts have emerged about the communion.

Before each play, the huddle enables the team captain to count the number of players that survived the last play. If a player is missing from the huddle, the quarterback calls for an immediate search of the field. Should it be the quarterback that failed to return to the huddle, sooner or later his absence is noted, because no one is saying anything. The other players must be alert enough to recognize the silent huddle as non-productive. Attempting to make small talk in order to cover an awkward lull in conversation degrades the purpose of the conclave.

When the quarterback, or any other player, crawls back to the huddle on his stomach, his participation is suspect. It behooves a team-mate to look towards the bench and point at the player writhing on the ground. The signal means "This player does not appear to be himself." It should be done behind the afflicted player's back, lest it be thought of as snitching. Unless the coach is too involved with his charts to notice, he will have the indisposed player removed from the huddle with all possible despatch to avoid having to take a time-out. The first-aid rule — do not move an injured person until he has received medical attention — does not apply to the football player on the field. So long as the player is conscious enough to express agony, he is hustled to the sidelines before his screams affect the confident atmosphere of the huddle.

Even more vital than its role as a place of reunion for the players, the huddle is where the quarterback calls the next play. It provides the privacy he needs. Football being a game of deception, the element of surprise is largely negated if the opposing team can overhear the play called by the quarterback. For this reason the huddle is held some distance behind the line of scrimmage: at least ten yards, farther if the defensive captain has unusually large ears and is known to sleep hanging from the roof of a cave.

To prevent having the signal read by the opponent, a quarterback should develop the ventriloquist's skill of speaking without moving his lips. Most quarterbacks also wear eye shadow to make it more difficult for the enemy to tell in which direction they are looking, but it may be a mistake to wear lipstick (see chapter nine, "Is Football Sissy?") The black quarterback does not paint white circles around his eyes, as this would remind people of old Tarzan movies and impair his authority in the huddle.

The confidentiality of messages in the huddle may also be destroyed by extrasensory perception (ESP), and more and more defensive team coaches are giving attention to including in their squad at least one linebacker with a sixty per cent or better average in intercepting thoughts. Unfortunately the player gifted with ESP often affects beads and one gold earring, and is less dependable during periods of the full moon.

To minimize leaks of classified information in the huddle, the quarterback uses a different signal to describe each upcoming play. A typical signal is "87 . . . red . . . left . . . hook," or "One if by land, two if by sea," or "Sighted sub, sank same." To understand what the signal means, each player must have memorized the play book. The play book is the equivalent of the Dead Sea Scrolls in his holy war against the foe. Once he is in the huddle it is too late to start deciphering the message, even if he has brought along an expert cryptanalyst. The player must study the play book in advance of the game. If he still does not understand the signal in the huddle, he should make a clean breast of the matter and ask the quarterback to call a number he knows, such as "Roll Out the Barrel".

The main point for the player to remember is: do not wait until you are in the huddle to decide whether you need extra tutoring in the form of a head transplant.

The last but by no means least function of the huddle is to afford *togetherness*. Some football coaches even tell their players to hold hands in the huddle. Although this means of supporting morale has lately come under a cloud (see chapter nine, "Is Football Sissy?"), a player may legitimately pat a teammate on the back if he is reasonably sure that the impact will not act as the *coup de grâce*.

It is in the huddle that the quarterback has the opportunity to express forgiveness to the players who missed their blocking assignments, with the result that the quarterback has more ribs than previously. He must exude confidence, though his team is losing 64 to 1. He leads the team in breaking out of the huddle, clapping his hands together and striding up to the line of scrimmage with the air of being perfectly satisfied with the relocation of his nose.

(NOTE: the player who refuses to leave the huddle, because it is the only safe place in the game, will be treated with the contempt he deserves. There is no room in football for the person who is morbidly preoccupied with self-preservation.)

"THE PLAY'S
THE THING"

Elevation (trio)

Shakespeare must have played an early form of football. His work abounds in references to the game. For example, the huddle is clearly alluded to in "The posteriors of this day; which the rude multitude call the afternoon" *(Love's Labour's Lost)*. " 'twas passing strange; 'Twas pitiful" *(Othello)* is the first critical comment on the aerial game, while offensive line play is found in "Once more unto the breach, dear friends, once more" *(Henry V)*. The passing formation — "Masters, spread yourselves" *(A Midsummer Night's Dream)* — and reading the defence — "By indirections find directions out" *(Hamlet)* — confirm that Shakespeare played for the Stratford Swans. Vince Lombardi himself could not have given more poignant expression to the special physical requirements of flankers: "There's a divinity that shapes our ends, rough-hew them how we will" *(Hamlet)*.

However, football has developed many more plays since the Bard devised the game plan "Every way makes my gain" *(Othello)*. The basic plays today include:

1. *The Sneak*. This play is used in short yardage situations where the quarterback does not trust anyone else to handle the ball, even though he is bonded. For this reason the Sneak should be used sparingly. When the quarterback calls Sneak after Sneak, and makes a scene when the referee takes the ball away from him to spot it for the next Sneak, the rest of the team becomes moody. Ball control is an excellent objective, but it can be overdone. The QB should therefore reserve the Sneak for those special occasions when he believes that the best way to gain the yard or two he needs is to follow the wedge of charging linemen and shoot himself into the air, to come to earth he knows not where.

The quarterback Sneak is not the prettiest play in football. Indeed, Europeans who see it for the first time have been heard to wonder aloud whether this was what God had in mind when He created dry land.

2. *The Running Play*. When the centre snaps the ball into the hands of the quarterback — as he must within twenty seconds or be penalized for being overly possessive — the quarterback is not required to keep it as a remembrance of their rather intimate relationship. He may hand the ball to one of his running backs. He should have reason to believe that the running back is expecting the ball. If the back runs right past him, without accepting the ball, the quarterback should check his deodorant. More likely however this is "a broken play".

Piling on

Social Response #1 Hitting

It is also very often a broken dream of reaching forty without someone having to cut up his meat for him.

What should the QB do when he finds that no one wants to take the ball from him except large persons wearing different-coloured jerseys? Should he A. hope that no one will notice that he is holding something besides his breath? B. quickly adopt the Quaker faith? C. hide the ball in tall grass and flap about pretending to be wounded?

Actually, none of these is correct. When unable to get rid of it in accordance with the play called in the huddle, the quarterback should "eat the ball". Does he literally eat the ball? If possible, yes. He will not have time to chew each mouthful eight times, as Mother told him to do, but indigestion is less distressing than six weeks of taking meals through a straw. The quarterback can begin training by swallowing the larger oval-shaped vitamin pills, and gradually work his way up through the junior-size to the regulation football. A light, dry wine is recommended when eating the ball.

More commonly, however, the quarterback merely *pretends* to eat the ball. He does this by falling on it, in the foetal position, as if receiving nourishment directly through the umbilicus. Thus sheltering the ball with his body, he prays that the opposing players who land violently on top of him will be penalized for "piling on", or attempting to perform an illegal abortion.

All going well, the hand-off from the quarterback to the running back is consummated. What, then, does the running back do with the ball? In certain rare situations he gives it back to the quarterback. The quarterback then throws the ball somewhere — anywhere — because he is seeing more of it than makes for a well-balanced social life. Fortunately, the running back more often retains the ball and runs with it. He may run with it in several different directions, though not all of them at the same time.

A. *Towards his own goal line*. A mistake. Although it is by far the most inviting prospect, since the area is much less crowded, ideal for a picnic or simply a quiet stroll across the verdure, it should be resisted. The points to be won lie at the opposite end. This is the direction of heavy traffic. The running back can get through the traffic more quickly by attaching a flashing red light to his helmet and making a noise like an ambulance (illegal), or by trying the following.

B. *The Sweep*. By running very hard, the back sweeps around the end of the line of scrimmage and proceeds downfield without being molested. That is the theory of the Sweep. In actual practice, alas, more often what is swept are the shattered bits of the running back, at the point of collision. Unless the opposing players have been blocked out of the action, one or more will greet the ball carrier as he turns the corner. This can give the ball carrier a lifetime phobia of turning corners, even when he is walking to the mailbox.

It is safe to say that football, more than any other game, demonstrates dramatically the gap between theory and practice, between the concept and the reality. The same play that on the blackboard embodies the philosophy of the perfectibility of man, on the field proves to be flawed, in much the same way that Custer's

Social Response #2 Interference

Social Response #3 Timing the miss

last stand was flawed. If every offensive play worked to perfection, every play would be a touchdown. Similarly, if every defensive play was performed exactly as it came to the coach in a vision, the ball carrier would suffer the ineluctable fate of being thrown for a loss. Football is therefore a game of disillusionment and excellent preparation for being a parent.

Initially however the ball carrier is expected to show a touching amount of faith in the intricate complex of blocking assignments that directly affect his longevity. It is essential that he believe that most of the opposing players will be knocked down by his teammates, leaving him a wide and pleasant vista in which every prospect pleases and only the referee is vile. If he also believes in the Tooth Fairy, all the better. He will have lots and lots of teeth to pop under his pillow, simply because infallibility is a property of the Pope and the Vatican City doesn't have a franchise.

On the Sweep or other plays, should the running back cultivate skepticism? Only if survival is a factor in his life plan. The most durable halfbacks, fullbacks, and ends are those who entertain the thought that something may go wrong on the play. Signals may be affected by sun spots. Opponents may not have heard of the Bill of Rights, which includes the right of the individual to life, liberty, and enjoyment of property. Hence the school of thought that says that the player should not be a martyr to dogma unless the head coach actually calls the plays from a burning bush.

In other words, the ball carrier may *improvise*. In moderation. When he gains good yardage "on his own" as "a solo effort" he risks offending the rest of the team. Everyone wants to feel needed. Generally speaking, therefore, the linemen prefer to see the ball carrier dismantled for a loss in which they have played an active role, rather than have him find a hole not of their making. True, his mates congratulate him when he returns to the huddle. They may even pat his behind. But if he does it again, in the same series of plays, the ball carrier notices a chill in the air that is not altogether autumnal. When he reaches for the towel hanging from the centre's belt, he may hear someone express surprise at his finding a use for another member of the team.

MORAL: football is a team game. It is better to lose the game as a team than to win it as a smartass.

C. *The Draw*. A mortality play. The Draw portrays the folly of letting one's blood lust get the better of one's judgment. In this play, the quarterback induces the charging opposing linemen to advance upon him, clawing the air and baring their fangs, then hands the ball to a back who runs through the hole vacated by the overzealous. Defensive linemen are so huge that, like supertankers, their ability to stop quickly depends upon their running into something. Deprived of an object to hit, the defensive lineman will continue to lumber indefinitely in the direction opposite to that of the run. This is why the Draw is considered to be a threat to the environment by Greenpeace and other organizations concerned about man-made disasters.

(NOTE: On this play, when the opposing linebacker sees what is happening he yells "Draw!" By then it is too late to affect the play, but, like the primal scream, it provides a focus for embarrassment.)

Social Response
#4 Basic blitz

D. *The Slant, Buck, Off-tackle, or All-Fall-Down-and-Go-Boom*. The coach sends in this play to chasten the running back who complains about not getting the ball often enough. The back tries to run through a hole made for him by the offensive line. This hole often resembles the black hole of outer space. That is, anything

Social Response #5   *Using the blocker*

sucked into it has an unimaginable density. The hole can reduce a 230-pound fullback to a pinhead. He may be bewildered to find that the void can have such a high occupancy rate.

But the basic principle of the play is sound: *a straight line is the shortest distance between two punts.*

To achieve this course the ball carrier runs "up the gut". It is not the scenic route (down the gut), but when it works he "sees daylight" (as opposed to having the lights go out). When he sees daylight — particularly if it is a night game — the ball carrier becomes very excited and runs towards it with the frantic, fixed resolve of all phototropic organisms.

E. *The Option.* In this play the quarterback, or occasionally a running back, carries the ball laterally, threatening to toss the ball to another back, or throw a forward pass, or dart through a hole, or tap dance his way into the hearts of millions. Unlike the back on the

Draw (also known as the drawback, though never to his face), on the Option play the back waits until the last second to make up his mind what to do. He has little time for meditation. If he has experienced difficulty in making decisions in relatively unhurried situations, such as choosing a laundry detergent, the Option may not be for him.

F. *The Double Reverse, Statue of Liberty, or Flea Flicker.* What all the running plays so far discussed have in common is that the ball changes hands several times, sometimes on purpose. Training drills for the Double Reverse include replacing the football with a hot potato. The quarterback tosses the hot potato to a running back, who tosses it back to the quarterback, who is so moved by this unselfish behaviour that he passes the spud to anyone whose need seems greater than his own — usually a defensive halfback. Hence the expression "He got burned on the play."

These complicated plays not only prove the validity of Murphy's Law ("If anything can go wrong, it will."), but they also make glowing testament to the saying, "It is more blessed to give than to receive." To receive a little too late is often no blessing at all.

3. *The Passing Play (Aeroballistics).* When the quarterback rears back and throws the ball as far as he can, it is one of the most dramatic plays in football. For one thing, the football flies through the air, where everyone can see it. For a few seconds the ball is clearly visible. This reassures the older spectators who haven't seen the ball since early in the season. And for the whole

crowd it is a treat to see something recklessly despatched by air to an uncertain destination without their having to pay the postage.

Passes come in a variety of lengths. The longest ("the Long Bomb") may travel as far as fifty yards in the air, enflaming passion in near-sighted pigeons and otherwise representing "a consummation devoutly to be wished". The percentage of consummations on this type of pass is, regrettably, on a par with that of a wild duck bent on making it with a Boeing 747. The flight is too demanding to result in a high degree of success. For this reason the Long Bomb is usually a desperation pass, attempted when the losing quarterback has tried everything else, including acupuncture.

Low-percentage pass

To improve the chances of the ball being received by the player for whom it was intended, or at least by someone in the same household, the receiver runs *a pattern*. The patterns run in football differ somewhat from the patterns turned out by Vogue. For one thing, the length required by the pattern (at least ten yards) is greater than that for a nightie, unless this is to fit a very tall lady. (That the coach is cutting out paper dolls has no real connection with the pass pattern).

The pattern run by the pass receiver serves the purpose of allowing him to "get open", a technical term meaning that he finds a place on the field where he can be alone, however briefly. The bliss of solitude celebrated by Wordsworth and Thoreau is compacted into fleeting ecstasy. The receiver who finds himself open rejoices in his isolation by waving his arms jubilantly at the quarterback, who all too often doesn't see him and throws the ball into the kind of crowd that attracts an accident.

The defensive backs show great concern that the potential pass receiver enjoy companionship. Some are so sensitive that they may actually weep for the receiver who has become lonesome. The defensive backfield coach takes infinite pains — most of them resistant to morphine — to ensure that, despite any natural shyness, the potential receiver is blessed with the society of people who share his interest in catching the ball. As a model of togetherness, family life finds an inspiring example in the coverage of football's passing play. Mom and Dad would never drift apart if they lived with a quarterback who threw them the baby on a down-and-out pattern. Such is the social message of football. Yet, sad to relate, many wives fail to appreciate the evangelism. They see their menfolk religiously watching football on television, but they miss entirely the sublime role of the game in bringing people closer together.

Despite the best efforts of all these caring people, however, a receiver does sometimes get open. How does he do this? He gets open A. by "putting a move" on the defensive back, or B. as the result of a defender missing an assignment, or C. thanks to clean living. The advantage that the receiver has over the defender is that he knows where he is going to zigzag and the defender doesn't, with the result that he may be zagging while the defender is still zigging. On no account should he tell the defender where he is going, regardless of how politely he is asked.

Deception is of the essence in football. The best football players are those who are masters at concealing their intent. This is why many of them go on to successful careers in politics. The game also provides a refuge from women. Every man knows that it is impossible to deceive a woman, even when phoning long-distance. Thanks to her female intuition, a female defender could tell not only which way the ball carrier was going to turn but also where he planned to spend the weekend and with whom. Mixed football therefore will doom the game as aught but an exercise in the obvious.

Working against males as gullible as himself, however, the quarterback throws the ball not directly at the receiver but at the spot on the field where the receiver is expected to arrive in the foreseeable future. This is called *anticipation*. When the receiver fails to show up it is of course an occasion of some embarrassment, comparable to that caused by the bride not showing up for the wedding. Some quarterbacks simply lack the confidence to throw the ball to someone who is not there. Sooner or later they weaken and throw the ball to someone who *is* there, but wearing the wrong jersey. Or they start imagining that they see pass receivers where there can be none — at the foot of the bed, for instance.

In this respect the football pass involves a technique identical to that of directing an unmanned spacecraft on a path to intersect with the path of a planet. Indeed the American space program owes a great deal to football. Once NASA stopped thinking of the moon as an inert lunar body and saw it as a wide receiver with a skin condition, man had as good as landed on the Sea of Tranquillity.

It is no coincidence that both the Houston space mission control centre and the frequently world champion Dallas Cowboys are neighbouring institutions. Not generally known is that early problems with the Apollo spacecraft were related not to pressurizing the capsule but to trying to lace it up. Similarly the Dallas quarterback is conditioned to launch a sideline pass programmed to make a soft landing on a flanker. No one was surprised that, when American astronauts Neil Armstrong and Buzz Aldrin hit the moon on the numbers their first impulse was to pick up an oval-shaped rock and run with it. The world saw only two Americans bounding about buoyantly in the reduced gravity of the

In Canadian football, all offensive backs may be in motion . . .

In American football, only one back may be in motion.

moon's surface, but people familiar with Texas football knew that inside their helmets the team was happy to be awarded the game ball 2160 miles in diameter.

Should the quarterback be fueled with oxygen before launching the forward pass? Yes. Oxygen is available from tanks beside the bench, though some quarterbacks can create the same propulsive thrust by exploding their bubblegum.

How much time does the QB have in which to achieve lift-off? Unlike the spacecraft at Cape Canaveral, the countdown for launch of the football does not begin twenty-four hours before ignition. On the contrary, the QB is fortunate if he has five seconds before the gantry collapses on him. He tries to postpone the inevitable by:

A. *Moving up into the pocket.* The quarterback's pocket in football is like the hip pocket in a girl's jeans: it doesn't hold much, it moves under pressure, and it attracts a hell of a lot of attention.

The quarterback who prefers to throw from the pocket is called a "drop-back" quarterback because he is dropped back there more times than he cares to remember. (NOTE: the drop-back pass should not be confused with the drop-out pass, which is a pass to a drop-out from an American college, a player who became eligible for the Canadian league because he flunked Nap Time.)

B. *Rolling out of the pocket.* The roll-out quarterback gives up the security of blockers who know where he is in exchange for mobility and the illusion that a moving target is harder to hit. The roll-out QB must be able to throw on the run, off either foot, or while being seated by an usher who does not wait to examine his stub. Obviously this style of quarterback needs strong legs as well as a strong arm, a large order since most experienced quarterbacks have knees held together with Krazy Glue.

C. *Scrambling*. The scrambling quarterback is much loved. He usually draws a large crowd to his funeral, as they expect him to find some way of scrambling clear of the grave. To scramble successfully, the quarterback must be able to survey potential receivers downfield while watching tacklers hurtling towards his body from all sides. For this reason it is an asset for the scrambling QB if he can move his eyeballs independently, like a lizard. This facility may frighten people (women particularly) in less violent social situations such as the church picnic, but tunnel vision is fatal to the scrambling quarterback, whose peripheral capability in seeing should be as close to 360 degrees as he can manage without restricting his training diet to insects. (If he also has a tail that regenerates when broken off, he should be grateful but should ask the team doctor to treat the matter as confidential.)

THE DEFENCE
(or Defense
or Whatever)

The Front 3¹/₂

The best defence is a good offence. Similarly, the best offence is a good defence. As this line of inquiry is not getting us anywhere, we can forget it.

The defence is the least understood part of football. The first, and the most important, factor in the confusion, is that nobody is sure how the word *defence* is either spelled or pronounced. Some people doubt that the word exists at all. These agnostics have usually had a traumatic personal experience on the football field during childhood, and they shield themselves by believing only in the words they see printed on the walls of railway station washrooms.

The preferred American spelling is *defense,* but the Canadian Press, before which all usage bows in the more northerly country, lays down *defence.* The question is: how long can the British spelling hold out against the American, which has had the benefit of a scholarship at a U.S. college? When *defence* is over-whelmed by *defense, offence* will promptly crumble under *offense*, and Canadian culture will once again be huddling in its own end zone.

Aggravating the Americanization of the game, the word is often pronounced with the accent on the first syllable: DEE-fense. Not de-FENCE. It is beyond the scope of this work to examine in depth the propensity of Americans to hit words in the first syllable (EYE-scream, CIG-aret, etc.). It apparently stems from an im-petuousness in the national temperament, plus an in-ability to cope with stress beyond the penultimate. Whatever the psychological origin, it sends a thrill of horror through Canadian philologists to hear a crowd of fifty thousand people at a CFL game chanting "DEE-fense! DEE-fense!" The only defence against this penetration by American usage is to put CBC and CTV sportscasters and colour commentators through vigorous verbal drills, the trainer treating every Americanism by taping up their mouths.

Assuming that it has been spelled and pronounced in the tradition of British fair play, what does the de-fence *do*? First, it tries to get the ball back for the of-fence. The defensive team can do this in several differ-ent ways:

A. *Getting a court order.* If the team can prove that it had legal custody of the ball at the time it was stolen, the judge may rule that the ball be turned over to the defence. Unfortunately this assumes that the defence is the natural mother of the ball, or has legally adopted it because the coach has no balls of his own. The ball is

112

often snatched while the team is "out to lunch". Deplorable though this is, restoring legal custody of the ball is often made difficult if the opposition has spirited away the ball from where it was last seen. Much as we must respect the due process of law, legal fees make it cheaper to knock the opposing quarterback's head off.

B. *Intercepting a pass*. It sometimes happens that a defensive back is able to step in front of the intended receiver and catch the ball. This is certainly an occasion. For one thing, if the back has the presence of mind to run with the ball, the defence has a chance to score a touchdown. When this happens the defence is highly elated. The defensive team rarely has the opportunity to see the ball close up, let alone touch it. There is therefore a natural temptation — which must be resisted — for the defensive back to show the ball to his wondering teammates, exhibiting the ball instead of running with it, flaunting it by waving it about, and generally displaying a lack of the quiet humility appropriate to being in the presence of divine revelation.

C. *Recovering a fumble*. There are two ways in which a ball carrier may fumble the ball. He may fumble it without assistance, as testament to being clumsy; or a defensive player may persuade him to fumble the ball, either by verbal message ("Drop it, Rover, drop it!") or by physically encouraging him to let go of the ball. Of the two methods, the physical is the more trustworthy. Indeed, inducing a fumble is not as easy as it may appear, because the ball carrier often has sticky stuff on his hands for the specific purpose of retaining the ball even after his arms have fallen off. Stripping the ball

113

The Interception

away may in fact require minor surgery. The local anaesthetic takes the form of a blow behind the left ear. When the ball squirts loose, the defensive player falls upon it with opposing players piling on top of him and trying to wrench the ball away, a scene that may partly explain why other civilizations in our galaxy have declined to respond to radio signals from Earth.

Should the defensive player put sticky stuff on his hands in case he recovers a fumble? No. Not unless he is very sure that at no point during the game will he pause to pick his nose. Playing out the half with one finger glued up your nostril is limiting, even hazardous. It also detracts from the aesthetic effect of the fumble when the players end up as a laminate.

Whatever the means used to cause the opponent to fumble the ball, it should be noted that a loose ball is like a loose woman: it takes a certain perverse delight in making a bunch of grown men look ridiculous. The harder the player falls on the ball, the more likely it is to squirt out, like a melon seed, and romp about the field with a demonic life of its own. Once it has been fumbled and enjoyed its freedom, a football is impossible to control and should be removed from the field, to be exorcised by a priest, if not actually destroyed.

D. *Denying the first down.* Failing the more dramatic event of the turnover, the defence can deprive the other team of the ball by not letting it get the ten yards it needs for a first down. This is a negative attitude, but nothing to be ashamed of. Many natural defensive players are born with a minus sign on their upper lip. Some grow a beard to cover it. They are being unnecessarily self-conscious. They are putting their negativism into a popular sport, instead of standing around blocking the aisle in a porno movie house, or acting moody because they were born too late for trench warfare. In football, refusing to budge is highly esteemed. But even greater glory is won by the defensive player who throws the ball carrier for a loss. This is a feat of brute strength, accomplished without fear of being shot for his tusks.

For every defensive lineman, the quality of mercy is not strained but droppeth like the quarterback.

The defence that drops the quarterback two or more times in one game knows a kind of ecstasy (the joy of sacks). It is on its way to earning a special name for itself: the Fearsome Foursome, the Purple People Eaters, the Orange Crush, the Edmonton Crude, the Sack Pack. These names bespeak the admiration of the community that the team represents. They suggest that the city has hair on its streets. There can be no questioning the virility of the population within a hundred-mile radius of the stadium. The member of such a defence attains the status of a folk hero, like the giant Paul Bunyan. Unfortunately, instead of accepting the company of a blue ox, he may be deluded by his press clippings to believe that he is strong enough to take a wife. He usually spends his declining years bellied up to a bar, waiting for someone to recognize him by his refusal to move.

E. *The special team*. When the defence balks at yielding the ten yards needed for a first down, the opponent shows his displeasure by getting rid of the ball. He may get rid of the ball in various ways. He may for

The Fearsome Foursome

instance put out a contract on the ball, the hit man waiting until the ball is sitting in a barber's chair, then blasting it with a shotgun. Or, if the goal posts are visible above the curvature of the Earth, he may try a field goal. Most often however he will try to dispose of the ball by using a punt. (A punt is a narrow, flat-bottomed boat with square ends, but this is not the punt used in football unless the field is really wet.) A football punt is a kick with the simple purpose of transporting the ball whatever distance will cause the receiver the most discomfort. Sometimes the receiver attempts to run the ball back. If he does so, he has an excellent chance of encountering the other side's special team, all of which is eager to meet him.

The special team is made up of players whose specialty is to self-destruct. They are often second-stringers who are strongly motivated to prove to the coach that their run from the locker room to the bench was not a fluke. They do this by knocking down as many people as

Converter   *Convertee*

Convertite   *Heathens*

possible, without discrimination by reason of race, national origin, colour, or religion. When successful, a member of the special team is rewarded by making the first team, posthumously.

To attain the velocity required for a truly impressive collision, the special team must get the adrenaline flowing quickly. The role of the adrenal gland in football is second in importance only to that of the salivary glands (spit). The adrenal gland quarterbacks the kidneys. It decides whether the player becomes a raging tiger or merely wets his pants. It fires up the whole body by producing steroids such as sex hormones and other secretions that enable the player to throw off 10,000 years of civilization. Because fast-flowing adrenaline is so essential to his transformation from a quiet Jekyll to a horrid Hyde, the special team player is especially careful to wear kidney pads that protect his pugnacity. This also makes the opposing special team feel better about hitting him from behind. Oddly enough, when this happens it is their coach's hair that turns white. His hormones have run into a penalty.

PENALTIES
(Allegiance
to the Flag)

Dead ball

Official's time-out

Football is a game that abounds in penalties. Penalties can hurt a team that is otherwise incapable of feeling anything. For this reason the coach tells his players never to commit an infraction of the rules unless they have exhausted all the possibilities of winning fairly.

Penalties are called by the football official. (Not to be confused with the official football, which is more symmetrical and often has better eyesight.) Football has more officials than any other game except tennis, which doesn't count because they are all sitting down. Having so many officials is a great blessing. Unlike soccer, where the referee makes all the calls and is frequently rewarded by being stoned to death by the crowd, football officials are numerous enough to be abominated as a group rather than individually. The referee (head official) often appears to be above the vulgarity of the rule violation. He listens with obvious distaste to the minor official's description of the foul committed, and assesses the penalty against the home team in a manner to indicate to the crowd that in the light of God's judgement the trespass call was picky, picky.

Nevertheless the crowd often boos the assessment of a penalty, or the failure to assess a penalty, timing its ululations to drown out the signal calls of the visiting quarterback. This is not very sporting. It is a kind of mob rule that has no place outside the legislature. The referee tolerates it only because it is preferable to the populist movement that would get him lynched from a crossbar. A low profile: that is the football official.

The officials are also distinguished from the players by the way they dress. Their pants are baggier, because they need pockets in which to carry their hankies. The official is lost without his hanky, not only because the coaches yell names at him that make his eyes water, but also because it is by throwing a hanky, or flag, that the official indicates that he has detected a violation of the rules. In other games the referee blows his whistle to stop the play, but in football the play is allowed to continue because the team offended against may advance the ball more yards than it would gain by taking the penalty. Or another official may spot a no-no and throw his hanky. In fact by the time the referee whistles the play to a stop the field may be littered with linen. This gives the officials a chance to get together (they sometimes get lonely out there) and compare notes. Offsetting penalties mean that the play must be taken over again. This pleases people who never had a second chance in life.

So the referee blows his whistle only when the play is dead. If a player is dead, he may blow it twice. When he blows it three times the referee thinks he is a railway locomotive and should be removed from the field at once.

Normally however the whistle means that the players must either stop whatever they are doing, or start doing it, whichever seems appropriate. The referee also stops and starts the clock by blowing his whistle. Thus he has power over both time and space, and his wind instrument is comparable to the pipes of Pan as the expression of a god: half man, half goat.

Football officials often live to a great age. This happens because avoiding players keeps them nimble enough to be able to walk through the stadium parking lot without getting run over.

In what deplorable circumstances does the football official hurl his hanky, besides that of hoping that a nice lady will pick it up and invite him to dinner?

A. *Offside.* The line of scrimmage has two sides: the *on* side and the *off* side. Unfortunately, unlike a light switch, the ON and OFF are not clearly marked. The restraining line, across which a player may not move until the ball has been snapped, is imaginary, not to say apocryphal. One day it will be possible for the line judge to lay a laser beam between the two front lines, so that the player who moves too soon loses his nose. This will reduce the number of offside penalties and encourage young people to take up plastic surgery.

In the meantime the penalty for encroachment is five yards, or half the distance to the goal line, whichever is the greater incentive to the coach to eat his clipboard. A quarterback who is old and wily may draw the other team offside by changing the cadence of his signal. Instead of barking "Hup! Hup!" as is his wont, he barks "Hup! Hup! Hup!" That is, his hup runneth over. The hazard in hupping thrice or more times is of course that one of his own players may be drawn offside. Or the quarterback may be unable to stop hiccupping and have to be carried to the dressing room, percolating loudly, and scared shoutless.

B. *No yards*. Because all life is sacred, the punt receiver may not be flattened as he is in the act of catching the ball. This is a rule of Canadian football often

forgotten by American players who have come into the Canadian Football League and who have yet to master the finer points of the game. The punt receiver therefore has a personal interest in the nationality of the players thundering towards him belching fire. Being able to recognize Americans may in fact be more relevant than at any time since the War of 1812. Landed immigrant status is meaningful when it's you the immigrant lands on.

In American football the punt receiver who does not wish to be particulated holds up his hand. In Canadian football this means only that he wants permission to go

to the bathroom. It can be safely ignored, since the first thing the player learns in training camp is to go to the bathroom before the game ("anticipation").

C. *Holding*. A team is penalized ten or fifteen yards, depending on the referee's religious background, if a player is caught holding an opposing player to whom he is not formally engaged. Usually it is a lineman who is guilty of this illicit intercourse. Unable to contain his man by the approved methods of butting, elbowing, slapping, or tripping, the lineman embraces his opponent and swears eternal devotion. Officials are quick to detect insincerity in the hug. Being men of the world, they can tell the difference between genuine affection

and a passing infatuation. When they do so they punish the offender by calling out his number. This turns the number into the Scarlet Letter and shrinks the lineman into a 270-pound midget. (There is no penalty for holding a player on your own team, at least not until your old woman finds out.)

D. *Clipping, or blocking from the rear.* An unnatural act, because it is done from behind. Some football texts refuse to discuss blocking from the rear because the book may fall into the hands of the impressionable. But not this book. It is better to risk shocking the reader than to have the player go out on the field, ignorance full-blown, and block from the rear, drawing a fifteen-yard penalty, possibly cancelling out a long run-back by a teammate, and bringing shame to his entire family. His parents may even disavow him, stating that they found him as a baby, left under their porch by dissolute gypsies.

Besides the moral implications, blocking from the rear can cause whiplash and jar the adrenal glands into giving buttermilk. Legal blocking is a case of full frontal crudity. Only if the other player is in possession of the ball may he be hit from any angle. If you are in any doubt, tap him on the shoulder and ask to see what he is carrying. If it is indeed the ball, then and only then should you break him in half.

E. *Grabbing the face mask.* This is an exception to the rule that the ball carrier may be brought to earth by any means that does not violate the SALT II agreement. The face mask is of course very tempting, providing something that the tackler can hang on to besides his religious faith. This is especially true when the ball carrier is the fireplug type, all thighs and eyeballs, presenting little on which the tackler can find purchase. Nevertheless the temptation must be resisted. Grabbing the face mask can result in serious damage to the helmet. The rivets, though sturdy, are not designed to take the centrifugal force of the wearer being whirled about the head like a slingshot, before being hurled out of bounds. There is also the chance that the tackler's fingers will lodge in the ball carrier's mouth, which is unsanitary. Fifteen yards.

F. *Roughing*. A subspecies of penalties called because of "unnecessary roughness". Often it is difficult for a football player to judge when his roughness is necessary and when it is unnecessary. A good example is provided by *the late hit*. Some hits are clearly late — after the ball carrier has been placed on a stretcher, for instance. But on other occasions it calls for very precise judgement to know when you are arriving late for the meeting. When the ball carrier already lies flattened on his face would appear to be a prime time to ram him, or to become the cherry on top of a people sundae. Piling on is frowned on, however, because of the ancient belief that it is unfair to hit a person when he is down. Common sense tells us that when he is down is the optimum time to hit a person, but some residual sportsmanship still exists in football despite efforts to bring the standard of pure meanness up to that of ice hockey.

It must also be remembered that the professional football player is a valuable property. Unlike other kinds of property, he is not worth more after he has been subdivided. On the contrary, though he may go on to a career doing television commercials for pantyhose or Absorbine Jr., the football league has lost a financial asset. It is therefore not surprising that officials are quick to punish a player for *roughing the passer*. The passer — usually the quarterback — is a very costly item. He cannot be replaced more than once or twice a season without crippling the club's budget, the most serious injury in football.

Thus the challenge for the defence is to quash the quarterback without appearing to want to do him bodily harm. A delicate execution. So much so, it is useful for the defensive player to practice on his mother while she is baking bread. Knocking her prone while she is looking the other way (blind-siding), and having her rather enjoy it as a reminder of her honeymoon: that's the trick. Also, master the aborted landing, flying over her prostrate form in order to crash on something inanimate. But do not hesitate to destroy her if she is stubborn enough to get to her feet while still holding the loaf of bread.

(NOTE: should you inadvertently sack the passer with undue brutality, be quick to offer your hand to help him to his feet. This show of courtesy may impress the official who would otherwise call a penalty because you broke the passer's collarbone. If the dazed quarterback refuses to let go of your hand after you have helped him upright, or if he asks you for your phone number, by all means knock him down again. Sometimes a penalty is unavoidable.)

G. *Throwing the ball away*. In certain situations,

such as when an opposing player is sitting on his chest, the quarterback will throw the ball away rather than lose yardage. When an official suspects that the quarterback has thrown the ball away, he calls a penalty. For this reason the quarterback rarely, if ever, admits that he has acted out of desperation. Instead he does his best to convince the referee that he is throwing the ball to a teammate who is visible to him alone. He shouts "Catch it, Leroy!" as he falls to the ground. He gets up astounded, like Macbeth after seeing the ghost of Banquo, that no one else has seen the apparition that was so obvious to his eyes. Luckily many football officials are very superstitious. They know that football stadia are haunted by the spirits of pass receivers who have gone on to the Paradise Bowl. Rather than risk offending the spectral presence, the official does not call a penalty for intentionally grounding the ball. Not when there is a chance that the quarterback has spotted a secondary receiver running a come-back pattern from the grave.

In order to improve his skill in passing to the disembodied, the quarterback should know something of the philosophy of George Berkeley (1685-1753), who denied the existence of matter. He maintained that material objects only exist through being perceived. Hence, it follows that the pass receiver is no more than an idea in the mind of God. Which means that he may or may not be near the ball when it is thrown, depending on whether God is thinking dump pass or sideline pattern. The quarterback must make it apparent that it is blasphemous to penalize an entire team just because the referee has a restricted view of the nature of reality.

Seldom-seen Official's Signals

Grounding the ref

Illegal laces

Offensive ball

Time-out

Roughing the language

Too long in the puddle

Loss of sense of direction

Loss of lunch

The quarterback conveys this by acting in a cool though hurried manner. Definitely suspect are 1. throwing the ball with the eyes shut, 2. screaming "Somebody for God's sake take this thing away from me!", and 3. lobbing the ball straight up (the burnt offering).

H. *Too long in the huddle.* Do not take advantage of a captive audience. The huddle is not the place to launch into the story of the funny thing that happened to you on the way to the stadium. The referee is bound to feel left out. If the team is ahead on the scoreboard, he is in a mood to suspect that it is attempting a ground game called "running out the clock", in which the entire team will limit its movement to shallow breathing. The referee then calls a *delay of game* penalty, which obliges the team to pack up its picnic things and move to a less desirable part of the field.

The proper way to delay the game is to take *a time-out*. In football each team is allowed three time-outs per half, during which it is supposed to remove its wounded from the field and repair damage to the environment. The coaches, however, tell the quarterback to save his time-outs until the last moments of the half, when it may be necessary to stop the clock in order to "keep the drive alive". Keeping the drive alive has priority over all other life-saving procedures. This is why an injured player is hustled off the field as quickly as possible without calling a time-out, even though his personal preference is to remain unconscious on the ground until the ambulance arrives. Willing hands whisk him to the sidelines, the applause of the crowd drowning out his groans.

To help preserve the time-out, the football player must develop a degree of stoicism towards pain. Trotting off the field on a broken leg may seem a severe test of your composure, but when the television or radio commentator has described the injury as your being "shaken up" it is not seemly to writhe on the turf demanding a sedative. In football, showing visible signs of agony is the exclusive privilege of the head coach. For the player to display actual physical suffering is in poor taste and can jeopardize his reputation for "playing hurt", which is as important as his doing television commercials for the United Way.

Canadian football has other ways of stopping the clock, especially on the prairies where the brisk winds can blow a cow into the scoreboard. The clock also stops when the ball carrier goes out of bounds, whether on purpose or because he has been caught in the undertow of the drainage system.

IS
FOOTBALL
SISSY?

The gay receiver

A cloud, no larger than a man's athletic support, has come over football. It was first noticed by television sportscasters who observed that many of the "moves" made by football players were as graceful and airborne as ballet. From this analysis it was an easy step to discovery that both football players and ballet dancers wear tights and are more emotional than people who play a man's game, such as golf. This in turn led to perceiving the linemen as the corps de ballet, the quarterback as the prima ballerina, and the coach as the choreographer — Diaghilev with cleats.

From the beginning, the resemblance between the two art forms (ballet and football) has been obvious in certain movements. For example, in both the basic contact is for one performer to seize the other around the waist in order to arrest his revolving. The only difference is that in football the revolving partner does not usually have time to twiddle his toes before being set down.

The kinship was not fully revealed however until a Canadian newspaper sent its ballet critic to write a review of a Grey Cup game between the Edmonton Eskimos and the Montreal Alouettes. Under the headline "Hark, Hark, the Lark", the ballet critic wrote in part:

> The story begins with the Eskimo huntsmen lined up on the field, eagerly awaiting the flushing of their prey. With a brave wave of his hand, their leader salutes the Magic Bladder. He then executes a dramatic *rond des jambes* that propels the Magic Bladder into the domain of the Lark. The Eskimo huntsmen rush forward joyously in search of anything that moves. They are enraged to find that the Magic Bladder has been captured by a Lark. There follows a lively *interlude*, Eskimo spearing Lark, and Lark soaring over Eskimo. This is very much a *divertissement,* a triumph of vigour over form.
>
> The Larks fail in their attempt to smuggle the Magic Bladder out of their own enclave, and lose it to the huntsmen. The Eskimo Prince (Tom Wilkinson) meets apart with his cohorts and enflames their fury by ejecting tobacco juice at a spot on the grass that is forever damned. The Prince then whispers a cryptic message that galvanizes his followers to trot to different places where, in unison, they put one hand to the ground to make sure that it is still there.
>
> The Eskimo Prince, a study in quiet resolution, moves in close to one of his larger huntsmen and

cups his hands under his behind. It is a moment of frozen poetry. Not by word or glance does he indicate that he suspects the presence of the Magic Bladder. Casting his gaze across the forces arrayed against him (furies snorting live steam into the frigid air), his mien reflects the confidence that says "Ask, it shall be given unto you."

He utters the secret word. At once, miraculously, the Magic Bladder appears in his hands. The Prince wastes not a moment on thanksgiving. He executes the classic *pas en arrière* (back pedal). Sensing climax, his henchmen hurl themselves forward, or sideways, in a paroxysm of devastation. They are clearly dedicated to the sacred mission of protecting and preserving the Magic Bladder, Death (hovering overhead in the ugly shape of the Press Box) being preferable to being put on waivers, an excruciating means of extinction.

Suddenly, the Magic Bladder is aloft! Transformed into an egg (Fertility), it flies impetuously towards its rendezvous with Fate. The Eskimo Prince pays a heavy price for this daring ascent of his egg into the laps of the gods. An exaltation of Larks, maddened by the profanity of the act, engages the Prince in an acrobatic movement that illustrates the truth that David's victory over Goliath was something of a fluke. The grace with which the Prince accepts the inevitable recalls to mind Milton's lines celebrating the casting down of Satan:

Dance of the Magic Bladder

From morn
To noon he fell . . .
    . . . and with the setting sun
Dropt from the zenith like a falling star.

And what of the Magic Bladder? Despite a magnificent *tour en l'air,* the defending Lark is unable to thwart the Eskimo huntsman's apprehension of the Magic Bladder while performing the exquisite *pas de bourrée* (progression on the points by a sequence of very small, even steps in order to stay in bounds; one of the most beautiful effects in football, suggestive of gliding). Carrying the Magic Bladder on high for all to see, the Eskimo carries it into the Enchanted End Zone, where he dances a droll *enchaînement* before slamming the Magic Bladder to the ground to symbolize the triumph of the spirit over artificial turf. The performance concludes with the Eskimo Prince embracing the captor of the Magic Bladder, and a grand *entrée triomphale* to the Nether World of the dressing room.

This interpretation of the football game as a pastoral ballet has encouraged the behaviourist to state that football gives homosexual males an excuse for bodily contact without the expense of renting a hotel room.

Writing in *Western Folklore,* anthropologist Alan Dundes of the University of California in Berkeley says that football is an erotic rite. He points out the "unequivocal sexual symbolism of the game" — the suggestive costume, complete with moulded codpiece, as well as the language of football ("score", "piling on", "rouge"). Dundes concludes that football is basically an effort by one group of men to subject another group of men to the sexual indignity of having their end zone penetrated.

Nonsense. While it is true that baboons assume a three-point stance to "present" their bottoms to superior males of the troop, the theory that millions of men make weekend widows of their wives by replacing normal sex with the spectacle of other males hugging one another and patting one another's bottoms — this is slander, dearie, nasty rotten rubbish.

If the gridiron is gay, what is the tennis court? With his grip on not one but two balls, his use of a stylized club (the caveman) to feminize the victim of the assault, and his vicious effort to hold his opponent to a "love" position, the tennis player is plainly perverted and Wimbledon should be renamed West Sodom.

However, the damage is done. Many a young man who thought that football was a manly game now fears that he will lose his virginity as he is bending over to recover a fumble. He is unsure where his pubic area lies in relation to the goal posts, and is afraid to ask. When a full-grown offensive guard blushes to see the tarpaulin removed, football is in trouble.

Players who once enjoyed the momentary respite of lying across an opponent's face now feel morally obliged to spring to their feet at once, hands extended to show that the tackle has involved no intimacy beyond a good-night kiss. Coaches are afflicted with a new problem: rookies who refuse to go into the showers without a

A weak-side run

chaperone. Instead of just giving their name to the referee they insist on showing him photos of their fiancées as proof of heterosexuality.

Formerly, there was no sexual implication when one team warned the other "We're gonna eat your a—s." It was treated as a figurative expression. Now however it is taken literally, an expression of carnal appetite. Younger players, when the time comes to get their a—ses off the bench, may try to take the bench with them. Even rephrasing the threat to "We're gonna eat your lunch," has not succeeded in convincing these rookies that what the enemy seeks to ravish is their peanut butter sandwich.

Further complicating the sexuality of football has been the introduction of cheerleaders whose scanty garb and provocative routines are likely to produce less cheers than heavy breathing. Alien beings observing a pro football game would be baffled to see Earthlings engage in a mass fertility rite in which its most sexually desirable females dance with wild abandon, and the huskiest males respond to the stimulus by all jumping on the smallest man on the field. If this is the way to sustain a dominant species numbering over five billion, the alien visitors might say, let's get the hell out of here.

It cannot be stated too categorically therefore: football is *not* a game played by eunuchs. The players are able to ignore the voluptuous cheerleaders only because they have tremendous concentration. Every player is heart and soul into the game. Also his coach has told him that if he looks at the cheerleaders his eyelids will fall off.

As for the spectators, the current state of sexual confusion in football has led some to believe that in order to enjoy the game they must be bisexual. This is alarmist. Being bisexual certainly helps, of course. But unless a person feels really uncomfortable watching football in mixed company, he has no reason to consider surgery.

Nor should we be made nervous by the theory that the reason men play and watch football with such emotional intensity is to compensate for their inability to bear young. In reproducing the species it is the female that carries the egg. The male — postulates the so-called Ovum Hypothesis of Football — frustrated in this vital function, finds an egg surrogate in the football (hence the shape). The male football player clutches the ball to his belly and runs with it in a frantic effort to duplicate ovulation. (Football players, too, have "good" days and "bad" days.) To assist in the delivery of the egg, the signal caller varies his cadence (the rhythm method). Even so, accidents happen. Sometimes a lineman finds himself carrying a ball even though he has been assured by the team doctor that the guard position is almost as safe as total abstention. When this happens, the best thing the player can do is either seek a legal abortion or go and stay with relatives out of town for a few months.

Plausible though the Ovum Hypothesis is, and despite the evidence that football players, after retiring from the game, develop paunches that would be a credit to any pre-natal class, it still fails to explain what football is all about. We may give it the same credence as we

give the anthropological *(The Golden Bough)* interpretation of football as basically a primitive rite of
autumn. It is simplistic to draw a parallel between
propitiating the grain god by slaying the Corn-Spirit
and killing the Rye-Spirit (Schenley).

No, what makes football essential to human life is
that it provides an outlet for territorial aggression without killing civilians. Football is the natural substitute
for World War Three. It is better to have the menfolk
kiss their women goodbye and march into the television
room than to march into a troop train. It may not be
possible to get the boys out of the trenches by Christmas, but the football season rarely extends beyond
January.

Where the equally decadent Romans made a mistake was not their placating the masses with bread and
circuses (hot dogs and football), but their failing to include the Huns and Visigoths in an interlocking
schedule. The wholesome thing about football is that
when British Columbia conquers Ottawa, the victors do
not rape the women unless there is a real demand. The
enemy is also destroyed with limited damage to build-
ings and property. The neutron bomb has, in fact, few
advantages over football, unless a fallout of Dixie cups
causes sterility.

Peace in the world will be secured when the NFL
and CFL have expansion teams in those parts where the
natives are still warlike without having recourse to
Howard Cosell. We need the Peking Dragons, the Mos-
cow Bears, the Saudi Camels, all working off their hos-
tility on the football field. That football is frequently

about as exciting as watching paint dry is irrelevant. It is a mistake to assume that a nuclear war will be more continuously entertaining because there will be no break in the action for television commercials. American scientists are even now modifying the Polaris missile to pause in flight long enough for a sponsor's message.

Canadians owe it to posterity to continue to be wildly enthusiastic about the Grey Cup. True, no one can say with certainty that the inhabitants of Carthage would have felt better about being pillaged had the occasion included the crowning of Miss Punic Wars. But without the emotional catharsis effected by the end-of-November spectacle of Grey Cup mayhem, the full violence of our bloody-mindedness would be unleashed in Christmas shopping.

Football. More than a game . . . a way of life . . . purging the primitive brute from men's souls . . . a communion with the basic nature of humankind. Hence the sacrilege in allowing stores to open on Sunday — the Lord's Day of football.

Blessed are the meek, for they shall have seats on the fifty-yard line.

A Completely Expurgated Glossary of Football Terms

Food bowl — the game as pronounced by a coach from
the Deep South

Pursuit — chasing the ball carrier long after he has
stopped caring

Time of possession — period during which a player won-
ders what possessed him to go near the ball

Scout — a snapper-up of unconsidered tackles

The bomb — an explosive device cleverly substituted for
the football while the opposition isn't looking

Blitz — a total assault supported by Panzer units

The dog — the blitz with tail back

Picking up the dog — blocker who also works for the
pound

Run the stunt — defensive manoeuvre resembling St.
Vitus Dance

Stun the runt — method of stopping a short halfback
with huge thighs

Fake hand-off — loss of an artifical limb

Broken play — play delivered by Canada Post

Tight end — tall player with a drinking problem

Clothes-line tackle — used by a team that can't afford a dryer

TDs — reward of a successful coach

DTs — reward of an unsuccessful coach

Flea flicker — player who flicks fleas on opposing linemen to distract them

Counter play — play called by a quarterback who wants to count the house

Turnover — made by folding one half of the team over the other half

Le ballon — the football on French television network (Football in French sounds suggestive. Parental guidance is advised.)

Great — most used word in football (SYNONYM: acceptable)

Wind — in Canadian football, what enables the quarterback to catch his own pass

Jargon Quiz   **Check one (at least)**

1. A receiver must have great
   (A) hands
   (B) tits
   (C) hopes.
2. When the ball carrier gets past the line of scrim-
   mage he can
   (A) see daylight
   (B) consider early retirement
   (C) scream for help.
3. As soon as he breaks into the open, the ball carrier
   turns on
   (A) the sprinkler
   (B) the after-burners
   (C) the eleven o'clock news.
4. The quarterback who evades a tackle has
   (A) dodged the bullet
   (B) ducked the rutabaga
   (C) wet his pants.

5. Running, the halfback shows
    (A) his private parts
    (B) respect for the elderly
    (C) blinding speed.
6. To show the intensity of its determination to win, a team
    (A) comes out throwing
    (B) comes out throwing up
    (C) comes out throwing a party.
7. Football is a game of
    (A) cubits
    (B) inches
    (C) nautical miles.
8. Under pressure, the inept quarterback throws
    (A) a wounded duck
    (B) a ruptured goose
    (C) a tantrum.
9. The pass is incomplete because the quarterback hit his receiver in a bad place —
    (A) on the fly
    (B) on the hands
    (C) on the road to Mandalay.
10. When both teams are hitting, you can really hear
    (A) the leather popping out there
    (B) the Mormon Tabernacle Choir
    (C) foghorns.
11. With a crushing tackle on an opponent, the player
    (A) wraps him up
    (B) eats him there
    (C) freezes him for later canning.

12. The team that plays aggressively has
   (A) come to play
   (B) come to the Lord
   (C) come to the aid of the party.
13. The team is also
   (A) up for the game
   (B) up for impaired driving
   (C) up yours.

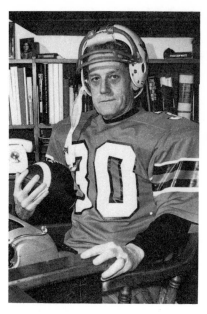

Eric Nicol
Nicol's place in the Football
Hall of Fame is the men's
room. Millions of visitors
have stood silently before the
white-tiled cairn, with its
intermittent play of waters,
in a moment of quiet tribute
to what this veteran has done
to the game of football.

(Nicol has given up active
football except for the teeth
guard, which still comforts
him as a pacifier.)

Photograph by
Bill Cunningham

Dave More
Although he lacks both speed
and agility, Dave More
continues to fumble his way
into the record books. He has
had some luck as a member
of the "specialty team" —
returning puns. When the
coach sends More onto the
gridiron, it's usually the
signal for a double-reverse
entendre, or the "end-around"
play. In one memorable game,
More intercepted three
limericks and a pack of
naughty postcards intended
for the team chaplain.

Photograph by Blair Pinder

160